ONCE UPON A DREAM

Cambridgeshire Poets

Edited By Warren Arthur

First published in Great Britain in 2017 by:

Young Writers
Remus House
Coltsfoot Drive
Peterborough
PE2 9BF
Telephone: 01733 890066
Website: www.youngwriters.co.uk

FOREWORD

Welcome Reader, to 'Once Upon A Dream –
Cambridgeshire Poets'.

For Young Writers' latest poetry competition, we asked our writers
to dig deep into their imagination and create a poem that paints
a picture of what they dream of.

The result is this collection of fantastic poetic verse that covers a
whole host of different topics. Snuggle up all comfy and let your
mind fly away with the fairies to explore the sweet joy of candy
lands, join in with a game of fantasy football, or you may even
catch a glimpse of a unicorn or another mythical creature. This
collection has a poem to suit everyone.

Whereas the majority of our writers chose to stick to a free verse
style, others gave themselves the challenge of other techniques
such as acrostics and rhyming couplets.

There was a great response to this competition which is always
nice to see, and the standard of entries was excellent. Therefore
I'd like to say congratulations to the winner in this book, *Envy
Louise Norris*, for their amazing poem, and a big thank you to
everyone else who entered.

Warren Arthur

CONTENTS

Ugne Stankute (8)	64
Maddison Sullivan-Andrews (8)	65
Alfie Milton (9)	66
Connor Knox-Brown (10)	67
Amy-Louise Lonergan (10)	68
William Hensby (10) & Joshua Peters	69
Jade Harris (10)	70
Kearia Blackledge	71
Robyn-Danni Turner (9)	72
Jake Forrest (11)	73
Gintare Ivanauskaite (9)	74
Grace Barden	75
Jimmy Hines (8)	76
Benjamin Spolander (10)	77
Mario Valentin Ciortan (9)	78
Dylan Green (9)	79
Cai Clapham (11)	80
Bethany Coenen (8)	81
Thomas Coenen (11)	82
Darci Adams (9)	83
Finley Walker (8)	84
Aiden Groves (9)	85
Elena Balaci, Alise, Katie Page, Lavinia & Adriana	86
Lily West (11)	87
Tajus Cicika (9)	88
Isa Hussain (10)	89
Kaitlin Martin (8)	90
James Murawski (9)	91
Lucas Ward (7)	92
Oliver Leon Ashley Profitt (8)	93
Nathaniel Slupek (9)	94
Colbey James Ring (11)	95
Mariya Owen (10)	96
Elias Williams (9)	97
Niall Grimshaw (11)	98
Rhyley James Canham (10)	99
Luka Baines-Howley (11)	100
Rhyannon Moisey-Clarke (10)	101
Cassie Faulkner (10)	102
Umar Mahmud (9)	103
Grace Hazel Zajac (11)	104
Melda (10)	105

Magda Stanczyk (8)	106
Bismah Hussain (8)	107
Isabella Rose Parsons (8)	108
Kaitlin Clark (11)	109
Reagan Morson (9)	110
Holly Christine (11)	111
Alice Bettany (8)	112
Brodiey Jack Ring (8)	113

Elm Road Primary School, Wisbech

Sophia Maderbocus (9)	114
Callum Malkin (10)	115
Kastytis Dambrauskas (9)	116
Alina Skok (10)	117
Henry Plume (10)	118
Henry Hussick (9)	119
Ruben Hughes (9)	120
Emilija Stonkute (10)	121
Emili Siskaite (10)	122
Bianca Martins (9)	123
Patrycja Snopek (9)	124
Sadia Ahmed (8)	125
Justin Woods (9)	126
Amelia Godfrey (10)	127
Edward Griffin Murrell (8)	128
Jenna-Marie Adams (8)	129
Leona Hobbs (8)	130
Amanda Mazure (10)	131
Alex Maniyathattu Binu (9)	132
Archie Wiles (8)	133

Kimbolton Preparatory School, Huntingdon

Lauren Cove (11)	134
Sammy-Jo Webb (11)	135

Kirkstone House School, Baston

Louise Lodge (8)	136
Honor Pearson (9)	137
Isabella Anstee (10)	138

Matteo Tamer Sadek (11)   139

Milton Road Primary School, Cambridge

Tilda Fox Holland (8)	140
Petar Cucakovic (8)	141
Maeve Talulla Shankar (8)	142
William Wratten	143
Loïc River Comment (9)	144
Genevieve White (8)	145
Isobel Mann (8)	146
Jassim Laoukili (9)	147

University Of Cambridge Primary School, Cambridge

Krishnan Thillai (8)	148
Monty Chatfield (8)	149
Vanya Ethan Fromant Skjodt (8)	150
Thomas Harrison-Zeronis (8)	151
Freddie Chatfield (8)	152
Willoughby Jones (8)	153
Isabella Wilkes-Read (8)	154
Alec Longden (8)	155
Alice Halsey (8)	156

West Walton Community Primary School, West Walton

Tristan Hicks (11)	157
Holly Walker (11)	158
Lorin Sahin (11)	161
Keira Evans (11)	162
Keira Lawrence (11)	165
Evie Lane (11)	166
Sonny Lee Sandberg (11)	169
Olivia Grace Reynolds (11)	170
Isabella Perks (11)	172
Evie Doughty (11)	174
Emmie May Parker (11)	176
Alfie Kierman (11)	178
Anderson MacCormick (11)	180
William Bates (10)	182

Phebe Helen Goose (11)	183
Lewis Taylor (11)	184
William Paul Hanslip (10)	185
George Buster Moore (11)	186
Lily Louise Gowler (10)	187
Darcey-Mae Jones (11)	188
Paige Markham (11)	189
Tristan Welby (11)	190
Shannon Harrison-Wiles (11)	191
Morgan Kirk (11)	192

Wisbech St Mary CE (VA) Primary School, St Mary

Olivia May Huggett (8)	193
Lillie Bardsley (9)	194
Blake Bevan-Black (9)	195
Kezia Sutherill (8)	196
Ashton Freddie Clarke (8)	197
Joshua Abrams-Stebbings (9)	198
Tiyanna Vanessa Lee (9)	199
Katelynn New (9)	200
Kalten McCarthy (9)	201
Max Waling (8)	202
Rhys Parrin (9)	203
Justin Ball (9)	204
Freddie Dearlove (9)	205

THE POEMS

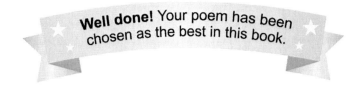

Well done! Your poem has been chosen as the best in this book.

Unicorn Dreams

Swishing tails, rainbow colours
I dream of unicorns
Fairy friends from Candy Land, some have just been born
Dancing round the unicorns are little tiny Smurfs
In the Coca-Cola sea, the tiny people surf.

Clouds as soft as cotton candy
My friend appears, her name is Mandy
I run through the long sugary grass
Looking at all the sweets I pass.

I love to be in this place
It always puts a smile on my face.

Envy Louise Norris (8)
Wisbech St Mary CE (VA) Primary School, St Mary

Soaring Through The Sky

I'm soaring through the sky
I can't believe it, I can fly
There's a robin called Gobin,
And a seagull called Deagull.
I fly faster than a plane, looking down
I see a crane.
Swooping and through damp clouds
Just beneath huge crowds
I'm soaring through the sky, I can't believe it I can fly,
But then an eagle called Meagle
Becomes jealous of my skills,
So he says go and I fall down with an enormous frown.
I try to fly but Meagle took my power.
Then everyone's like, 'Look, he's falling at ten miles per hour!'
Then I was cowering.
I got a spark of flight and I said, 'I must get up there!'
So I flew as fast as a swimming shark.
Meagle had gone and I was free
I'm soaring through the sky,
I can't believe it, I can fly!

Kaden Lack (11)
Discovery Primary School, Walton

Fairy Kingdom

As the day grew bright
The enchanted kingdom was dazzling with the bright
colours of the rainbow
Which stood on top of pink fluffy clouds.

As I flew through the sky, I stopped and gazed around
I noticed how beautiful the kingdom of rainbows was.

I went inside the castle and there
I saw the beautiful fairy and her pet unicorn Rainbow
Dash.

The three of us had golden hair
That shimmered in the light of the dazzling sun
Which was up high in the sky.

My emotions began tingling inside,
I felt happy, I felt amazed and I felt emotional
But most of all I have enjoyed my journey through the
sky.

Sadly all dreams have an end.
However, as I waved farewell I did not feel sadness
But excitement, for I knew I would have this dream
again.

Carolina Baiao (8)
Discovery Primary School, Walton

My Unicorn Dream

I gallop silently through the night
On my unicorn friend, all shiny and bright
I am here in the world of imagination
Oh look over there, it's the dream station
I dream of unicorn dust in the night sky twinkling
Until the master of unicorns looked at me with his eyes wrinkling
'Hello sir,' I salute
With his horn stood straight like a flute
His wings glistening as he flew
His long and curly hair a navy blue
Then I realised my heads started to ache
While smelling the scent of tasty steak
I wake up rushing downstairs
Finding lots of navy-blue hairs
I head towards the table after an adventure in the World of Imagination
As I find the sparkling dust from dream station
My heart was pounding as I knew
That my unicorn adventure was really true!

Tia Nikita Harley (10)
Discovery Primary School, Walton

The Dark Night

One frightful night I appeared in a pitch-black cave
I was feeling brave because
I started walking in the dullness of the place
I finally spotted a room with a light on
I wanted to peer inside so I tiptoed
When I got closer and closer
Huge spiders came out of nowhere
I stopped myself from screaming
Then I quickly walked past them
I found myself in a room with deadly potions
Suddenly, an old man with a grey beard
And an ancient walking stick started creeping up
behind me
Then I spotted an open door to a room
There were more old men who had potions in their
hands,
Then they threw one at me
I became one of them.

Jack Parbles (10)
Discovery Primary School, Walton

Last Night I Dreamt...

Last night I dreamt that I was an Olympic gymnast
Back handsprings, front flips, all those epic tricks
All those events, bars, floor, beam, bar,
Vault and trampoline.

I had a sparkling leotard with white jewels
And everyone was shouting my name
I felt amazed and scared at the same time
If I didn't get it right
I felt I would feel like I would let everyone down.

Everyone was depending on me...
This is the moment...
When I'd finished my floor routine,
Everyone was roaring with happiness.

Finally, my name got announced for gold!
Then I woke up and remembered it was all a dream.

Liliana Bates (10)
Discovery Primary School, Walton

Being A Footballer

F ootballing is some people's dream job, it is for me ever since I was a toddler

O nce when I was a little boy I was talent scouted and it gave me confidence in myself

O n 27th February, I played my first football match for Cambridge United and won MOTM

T hat gave me the most confidence ever, it made me think I could be a professional footballer

B eing a footballer makes you think it's easy

A ll of the footballers must be really good which makes me think I am really good

L oving football is good because it is the most exciting sport in the world

L ove football, love sport, love Great Britain.

Tyler Downing (9)

Discovery Primary School, Walton

Dreams

O nce upon a dream, always a dream
N o one can stop having a dream
C lever people know that
E ven I know that!

U nknown people even know that
P eople always have a dream
O h! I am having one right now!
N o one always has nice dreams

A lthough lots of people have some nice dreams

D id I have a nice dream?
R ock 'n' roll, what did you dream about?
E veryone can have fun in a dream
A happy place or an angry place, I don't know
M aybe a scary place, well keep on dreaming.

Roxy Ximenes Belo (9)
Discovery Primary School, Walton

The Unicorn's Charm!

A beautiful being, enchanting and pure
As white as a lily, so proud and sure
With a silvery mane that flows in the breeze
And eyes that bewitch you and makes your soul freeze
But in an instant, her eyes seemed to change
And so melts the ice, causing feelings so strange
Straight to your heart the warmth travels but slow
And both captive and unicorns seem to shine and glow
Here something passes between the two like a trance
Causing Dry and Nymph to awaken and dance
The unicorn talisman that pearly white horn
That this beast is perfection is chosen to adorn.

Emily Green (10)
Discovery Primary School, Walton

The Land Of The Royal

L and of the Royal here I come
A queen I should be in this fantasy
N o, I will not leave
D ogs run around the tree.

O h, I love you and you love me
F un lays underneath.

T o meet you, what a treat
H aving tea with the Queen, what a delight
E verything in my world is bright.

R oyalty is my name
O h call it, I'm like your dame
Y ou are not alone because I'm always by your side
A ll you gave me is too much
L oneliness is not true 'cause I am always with you.

Aliya Tahir (8)
Discovery Primary School, Walton

My Nightmare Rabbit

R emember my dream?

A bout a cute rabbit

B ut it was no ordinary rabbit

B ut a rabbit that turned into a very scary rabbit

I t liked to eat children, especially little ones

T his rabbit liked to play hide-and-seek but beware, chomp, smack, a child is gone

D o try to hide but he'll find you no matter where

R un as fast as a cheetah, he will still overtake you

E at, that's all he wants

A t midnight he comes out to eat

M idnight, try to hide under your covers and don't breathe you might not get caught.

Evelina Markeviciute (9)
Discovery Primary School, Walton

Sugar War

Bang, I lay down upon the ground
Weird voices shouting, 'Get down, get down!'
A sweet smell filled the atmosphere
And out of nowhere came a candy cane spear

I stood up, looked around, saw two teams of chocolate
Two candyfloss castles and a caramel handle
Ice cream catapults, lollipop machine guns
Dark and white chocolate soldiers, tonnes and tonnes

What a day, haven't seen one quite like it
A candyfloss castle, might have eaten a bit
I woke up in my bed, and here I sit.

Oliver Barden
Discovery Primary School, Walton

My Fear Of Bows

M y dream was extraordinary
Y ou see this was odd

D reams are my place where I eat cake
R ed icing went crackle, crackle
E d is my favourite because he has
A lways got a smile
M onday when I came something was odd

O f course there was cake but it was cold as ice
F or a while I thought I was in a fridge

A ll of a sudden puff, puff

B ows surrounded me I curled in a ball
O h no I woke up
W hen I next sleep I am going to put my bow away.

Scarlett Louise Williams (8)
Discovery Primary School, Walton

His Dream Lives On

Today is the day we all sing
In honour of Martin Luther King
Wherever people fight to be free
His name is remembered with dignity
When black people weren't treated right
He stood strong to lead the fight
He fought with love, not guns or darts
He changed people's minds and their hearts
But some people didn't like his words
He was taken away to a better world
Yet his dream lives on that all can be free
When we knock down the walls
Between you and me
Martin Luther King's life did not last
But his dream and his spirit are free at last.

Hifsa Iqbal (10)
Discovery Primary School, Walton

Fantasy Land

As I drifted away to fantasy land
I dropped on the grass and I started to stand
In the bog there I saw
Shrek and his friends
And stomping round Peppa Pig too
The hippogriff soared over, high in the sky
And the Gruffalo sat on the loo!

'Off with his head!' the Queen of Hearts screamed
As the flash zoomed by with glee
The BFG towered over the land
And Dobby got stung a bee!

The three blind mice burst with laughter
As I sat there eating ice cream
I drifted away back to Earth
And I realised it was all a dream!

Shreyan Pankhania (10)
Discovery Primary School, Walton

In My Dream World

In my dream world wizards and witches cast spells
The monsters build magic wells
In my dream world I have a sparkly pink unicorn
With a long, swirly enchanted horn
Wait, there's more in my dream world.

My dream world is enchanted
I saw a dog that panted
Oh no there's that pirate he's as mean as they come
But his crew is very dumb.

In my dream world ogres and giants exist
They live in the part where there's mist
In my dream world I met the Queen
I told her don't be scared of the monsters, they aren't mean.

Matilda Rose Hookham (7)
Discovery Primary School, Walton

Never Give Up

I am a gymnast, as strong as could be
I'm too scared to try
Too scared to compete
But when I found out I had to compete
Suddenly, I wanted to quit
Then my coach said, I will help you
Suddenly, I didn't want to quit.

I trained hard for when I compete
Then the time came, I had to compete
I started well, then I fell
How disheartened did I feel
I carried on until I was done
Then I heard my score
I couldn't believe my eyes, I got a nine
That is why you should never give up.

Kelsey Mitchell (11)
Discovery Primary School, Walton

Archery In America

A mazing day today in America
R ainbow is above me, will I be lucky?
C reatures are with me
'H ave fun,' Dad said
E very step I take everyone is with me
R eally I can't believe my eyes, it is the royal family
Y ou can't defeat me

I n America it is hot
N ot my favourite day

A m I going to win?
M eet new people
E nergetic day
R ide on a train
I n a dream
C elebration
A n American dream!

Cheyanne Susan Kathleen Ferreday
Discovery Primary School, Walton

A Life's Dream

On the day I was awoken
My sleep I had fought
When I opened one eye
I had a great big thought
Why am I on the clouds?
Why is there ocean everywhere I go?
But then I saw a unicorn
I jumped on its back
'Let's got to Narnia,' I said
The unicorn was called Riley
He was angry
And rather posh
I said, 'Where's the closest house?'
'Oh Master, we only have castles.'
'Please take me to it.'
I saw Jimmy and Martynas!
I awoke with a fight
In my mum's arms safe and sound.

Kelsey-Mai O'Sullivan
Discovery Primary School, Walton

Oh My Unicorn

My unicorn, my unicorn
Where have you been?
I've been looking all night
But you were not in my sight
You're the most gorgeous thing I have ever seen!

You were not in the forest
You were not in the farm
You were not in the bushes
And you weren't in the barn!

And then I saw you.
Finally! At last!
Your shiny white skin
Your flashy hair, flashy like glass.

You are now with me
Cuddly and warm
We go where we belong
To home sweet home.

Maria Brozyna (9)
Discovery Primary School, Walton

A Dragon's Revenge

I open my eyes
I'm confused and tired
I see piles of bones and broken buildings
Nothing around but fire
I hear loud noises
I see a dragon fly by.

A dragon swoops down at me
It crashes into a building as I take cover
It begins to blow fire everywhere
More dragons arrive
Destroying everything in sight
Taking the city by force.

They start to get closer to me
Slowly walking to me
Looking even more scary, every step
It gets dark then I wake up in my bed.

Aaron Goulding (11)
Discovery Primary School, Walton

The Magical Forest

I lay on my pillow
I had fallen asleep
I was alone in the wood
Just a normal wood
Frozen by fright
I spot a glistening glow
I scrambled to see what it was
A magical forest opened up around me
A fairy appeared
Taking my hand, together we flew high in the sky
Soaring like a bird
In my mystical woodland below
I spotted a group of beautiful ballerinas gracefully pirouetting
We floated down and danced with them until dawn
Stirring from my sleep, I wondered had it just been a dream?

Mollie Osborne (8)
Discovery Primary School, Walton

The Breezy Snowflakes

S nowflake dancing while it floats down to the ground

N othing else except ice and water is in snow

O nly if you step on it does it go, only hot things melt the snow

W hile snow floats down the air is cold

F eel like you want to go out in the snow?

L ove snow, but don't eat it

A snowflake is beautiful, it is graceful and elegant

K ings can't control the weather and neither can queens

E legantly, the snowflakes come down.

Catherine Mai Runacres (8)
Discovery Primary School, Walton

Horse Racers

H ere I come to be professional
O n the way to win the race
R ight on the line, I win
S omewhere behind me the racers chase
E veryone is cheering for me the way I go

R attling horses trotting behind me
A m I going to win?
C ompete against each other, sorry for them
E veryone gathers round me
R ather give my trophy to the person that fell
S orry for everyone who couldn't beat me... or would
they?

Jack Benjamin Sharpe (10)
Discovery Primary School, Walton

Once I Had A Dream

Once I had a dream
Where I was swimming in a pool of cheese
And then a computer started to sneeze

Once I had a dream
Where pencils started to sing
And all the rubbers went *ding*

Once I had a dream
Where cannons fired sweets
And swords were made out of meats

Once I had a dream
Where rabbits had a race
To see who was the first rabbit to go to space

Once I had a dream
Where I was writing a poem about my dreams.

Sophie Warren (7)
Discovery Primary School, Walton

My Story Powers

I'm in a dream castle far away
It's as gold as hay
No one knows if I'm going to stay

I'm trapped in a wire
It's full of fire
Will a knight
Save me or will I fight?

I hear a creepy sound
And it's twice as loud
I turn around and I know
It is Liliana, she's doing
Somersaults and flips
She's an Olympic champion
She's won lots of golds
Finally, I woke up, I remember it was a dream.

Yana Chamapiwa (9)
Discovery Primary School, Walton

Unikitten And The Midnight Garden

I have a kitten
That loves to play
In the night sky that makes glee
She gives me a fright sometimes
That leaves me in the deep pitch-black darkness
I see shadows
That seemed familiar
I walk up to it
But wait, it's my buddy and my kitten
We all play in garden
Feeling quite happy
My unikitten loves me
And I love her
We tell our wishes to our kitten
That come true
It's starting to be day so I need to go
I have to say my cat is magical.

Wiktoria Wyrostek (11)
Discovery Primary School, Walton

Football Greats

F rank Lampard played for Chelsea

O h you've got to know

O h London is where I am

T ake the journey with me to see who I meet

B obby Charlton

A h my goodness, it's Pelé!

L ewandowski is 4th and the only polish man on the list

L egends, legends, and more legends

E den Hazard, another Chelsea hero

R ooney and Rues start with Rs

S o here's the best two: Lionel Messi and Neymar Jr.

Riley Morson (10)
Discovery Primary School, Walton

My Candy Land House

I live in a castle fit for a queen
I'm rich and famous
The reason why I'm rich and famous
Is because I am a queen of Candy Land.

In my castle fit for a queen
I have a stable for my pet unicorn
My pet unicorn is the name of a flower.

My house is in the Land of Candy Land
And is made with cupcake walls and a chocolate door
with
Windows of pink rock candy.

Above my castle, pink and white clouds float in the
bright pink sky.

Ellie Miller (8)
Discovery Primary School, Walton

The Crazy Zoo

It's a sunny day at this crazy place,
Being at the zoo puts a smile on my face.
I'm drinking my sippo,
I see a hippo.
There's a lion called Ryan and a chick called Mick.
There's a family of giraffes wearing knitted scarves.
The monkey is dancing funky.
The pig is doing a jig.
The snake is in a lake.
The bare bear had no hair so he couldn't scare.

We've had a fun day at the zoo
But watch out, the gorillas are throwing poo!

Lauren Lack (8)
Discovery Primary School, Walton

Candyland And The Nightmare

Last night I was in Candyland
it was dark and spooky
Suddenly, amazing lollypops were right in my face
Suddenly, it all lit up
Then I became the Queen of Candy Land
The I found out I have powers
I could eat candy whenever I liked, but that was not my power!
My power is to raise the sun and put it down again.
I could also defeat evil
One day I tried to raise the sun, but it didn't work.
All the candy was wondering what was happening
it was pitch-black.

Chanelle Anne Epathite (9)
Discovery Primary School, Walton

Violent Volcanoes

V olcanologists study volcanoes day by day

O range and reds rule the sky

L ava dribbles down the sides

C rack, the edges split like leaves burning in a fire

A sh and melted rock runs down the sides like thick treacle

N ever ending columns of purple ash shoot into the night sky

O ver and over again the volcano erupts viciously

E ruptions cover the lands of Pompeii

S himmering crystals fly in every direction.

Alina Rasul (9)

Discovery Primary School, Walton

Hogwarts

H ow did I get invited here?

O n the weirdest castle grounds

G irls and boys wearing cloaks and carrying books

W itches and wizards casting spells all around me

A t the girls' common room I see Hermione Granger

R unning away from Dementors as black as coal

T he witches and wizards try to defend the castle

S uddenly, I woke up safe from casting spells all day!

Amber Louise Wright (11)
Discovery Primary School, Walton

My Journey On A Unicorn

My journey on a unicorn in the night
Then I realised it was afraid of heights
Looking down at the cotton clouds
It looked like a crowd.

I can see a bright purple horn as swirly as a beautiful
snail
It's bright rainbow hair and beautiful swishing tail
Can be spotted far, far away
In the light of day.

I see the sun
You were very fun
And I know it is time to say goodbye.

Neja Teiserskyte (9)
Discovery Primary School, Walton

Fairy Magic

F airies all around me
A pple houses hanging in the trees
I can see their glittering wands as the slip past me
R ound and round in the moonlight they go
Y ou can see them too

M agic's in the air
A little fairy door in a big oak tree
G low worms light the door for everyone to see
I can see their sparkly wings as they fly through the woods
C an you find them too?

Lorna Taylor (8)
Discovery Primary School, Walton

Sea Unicorn

S hining coat of glistening white
E nergy surges through its body so bright
A sleep all day and galloping all night!

U nimaginable portrait of beauty
N eighing its heart out, ever so pretty
I llusion it is definitely not
C harming manes without a single knot
O verpowering people like you and me
R acing over the horizon to be
N ot a care in the world this unicorn has.

Malaika Rasul
Discovery Primary School, Walton

In My Dream Land

In my dream land
There are candyfloss trees
And lovely pink and purple bees

In my dreamland
We'd go to the park
Then have a race
Everyone would be a winner
And I'd sit in the spinner

In my dream land
Bears wouldn't have hairs
In my dream land
The sun could smile and be seen from a mile

In my dream land there would only be sun
And of course fun
Everyone would love a bun.

Rihanna Janet Dyer (8)
Discovery Primary School, Walton

The Scary Crew!

In the scary crew there were five incredibly frightening
Halloween monsters
The dumb one was the zombie,
The smart one was the vampire
And the funny one was the wolf
The most mean one was the scarecrow
And the skeleton was the scariest one.

Fred was as dumb as a giant
He'd never get the job done
Vee was the smart one but she always had a thirst for
blood
And a huge appetite
The others didn't have a lot to talk about.

Yasmin Ella Howell (9)
Discovery Primary School, Walton

Famous Singer

F amous I wish to be
A m I just so silly?
M ost people don't know I sing
O nce upon a dream I wear such bling
U pon a stage
S hining bright

S tar tonight
I n my dreams
N ice it feels as they shout my name
G etting closer to my dream
E ars listening
R eally! I think I've done it.

Abi Stafford (10)

Discovery Primary School, Walton

Stars

S tars silently dance in the day

T hen when the day is over, day turns into night

A nd they go as stiff as a storybook.

R ing-ring the doorbells go as a present arrives for me. I unwrap it gently and as I unwrap it I know what it is. A telescope! I race to my window and look at the stars. I notice how they always dance and prance, before I just could not see

S tars are beautiful, stars are bright and they shine in the night.

Amy Taylor (8)
Discovery Primary School, Walton

The Rainbow Unicorn

R ainbow in your hair
A ruby in your eye
I would like to fly
N o, please don't leave
B e with me
O nly because we are buddies
W ill you stay?

U nder you is a cloud
N othing can take us apart
I will stay with you in your life
C lara you will be
O nly because you are mine
R unning to your house
N ever I shall leave.

Elena Doveikaite (9)
Discovery Primary School, Walton

Killer Clown Knocking

K iller clowns always knock
I would like to tell them to stop
L et the clock tick
L oaves of bread falling through the ceiling
E ntry is not today
R emember what happened yesterday

C locks ticking one hour fast
L ocks are clicking
O wls are howling
W onder when this day will end?
N erves are getting mad
S erious, this is getting mad!

Lennox Richardson-Owen (8)
Discovery Primary School, Walton

Nightmare

N othing there but creepy noises
I walk downstairs, nothing there
G lancing everywhere, there is me
H ow did I get here? Is this a joke?
T hud! What noise is behind me?
M y worst nightmare is a bat clown
A mystical creature is running and coming!
R unning like a cheetah his name is Peter
E erie eyes glow, close my own in dread
S uddenly, I wake up at home.

Martins Liepins (10)
Discovery Primary School, Walton

The Candy Land

The candy land was full of colour, full of rainbows
And proud clouds dancing in the blue sky.
The houses are made out of different kinds of sweets,
Jelly beans, Smarties and Twix walls
My house is made out of toffee,
It has cute-looking jelly babies and yummy candy canes.
The roof has bluey frosting with Smarties
The garden is full of sugary things.
KitKats, Sour Patch Kids, cream eggs and so much more!

Zuzanna Wiktoria Chlopot (9)
Discovery Primary School, Walton

The House Of Wonders

Last night I dreamt
I lived in a golden house
Also, it was made of diamonds
The windows were pink stained glass
And the door was brown rock candy
before I lived there I lived in the poorest house anyone
could live in.
I went to bed one day and when I woke up
I found myself united in the richest house in the world
I was very confused when I woke up
I wasn't where I used to be
And loads of people knew me.

Lola Rose O'Malley (9)
Discovery Primary School, Walton

Speed

I saw land and it saw me
I walked up to the tree
But can it be?
I saw a tree that had electricity with static.

A wizard was in a fight
He was using all his might
But then he came
Everyone knows his name.

He took me to his lair
But I don't know where
I was in an attic
With a statue.

I saw a hook, then the deserts shook
As an earthquake hit the cook.

David Akehurst (10)
Discovery Primary School, Walton

The Candyland

Once upon a dream, I landed in some cream.
Finding myself in Candyland
Candy canes for trees?
Is this what I see?
I met some friends,
Their names were Sugarbun and Bunny Pop
Finding myself in Candyland,
Lollie and Emma had disappeared
They were stuffing their faces with candy canes
I said, 'Come on girls, haven't got all day!'

Laila Smith (9)
Discovery Primary School, Walton

The Terrific Dreamland

This world is upside down
And the clouds taste like candyfloss
I said to myself, 'Where am I?' I was so confused
I saw candy canes growing as fast as a flash
Then I saw a monster having a feast
He was sad
At least he was enjoying his feast
A tree was growing
Out some crisps
Then I was eating the delicious crisps
The sun was shouting at me
He really wanted crisps.

Abdulraheem Qureshi (9)
Discovery Primary School, Walton

Unicorns

As I arrived
It seemed to call my name
Flowers, it seemed to rain.

As I strode further in
I sensed some movement
Then I heard a crack
I looked around.

When I saw a cloud of sparkling dust
Fairy dust in fact
I knew it was a magical place.

Then I walked forward to see
A fairy surrounded by magical unicorns.

Emily Shadwell (11)
Discovery Primary School, Walton

Me And You

I fall to the ground
A cloud catches me
An enchanted forest it seems to be.

I open my eyes
To see a small speck of light
That grows more bright
So close, yet so far
A rainbow unicorn emerged
It felt so bizarre.

It offered a ride up to the sky
And we rode through the galaxy
Just you and I.

Anastasia Piekarz
Discovery Primary School, Walton

Santa's Unicorn

There you stood amongst the brightly lit
Christmas trees
your shining brown eyes
Stared at me confusingly.

You had glistening hooves
That shone in the crystal-white snow
And your candyfloss hair
Flowed in the wind.

Your candy cane horn
Cutting through the wind like a spear
The white of your horn camouflaged
In your white silky coat.

Amelia Dawn Wright (8)
Discovery Primary School, Walton

Science

My lab coat is as white as snow
The tails of my lab coat are dancing
Through the cold winter wind
Rushing through the open door
My goggles are so see-through
Like a crystal-clear sea
My experiments fizz, bang and pop
Like crazy, colourful fireworks
With hard, heavy jars sitting on the shelf beside me
Containing sparkly, magical chemicals
My excitement bubbles.

Imogen Grooms (9)
Discovery Primary School, Walton

Dreamland

Once, I'd really like to go to Dreamland
In Dreamland you can have a spooky or wonderful
dream
Dreamland is a beautiful land like Disneyland
Dreamland has a toffee chimney that you can even
have some coffee
When it's night you can see the lights on the chocolate
roofs
Lights are bright like the shiny, sparkly stars
The door to Dreamland is made out of delicious
chocolate.

Nela Batiova (9)
Discovery Primary School, Walton

My Dream Life

Dream, dream
My life is running slow
so hurry up dream,
Where are you?
Dream come to me
wherever you are
come, come.
Some day, I want to be a writer!
A famous, joyful writer.
I can see my dream
in a cotton candy house.
A unicorn big or small
running drown the street laughing loudly.
This is my dream
My bestie Lily is in my dream too!

Davina Martin (11)
Discovery Primary School, Walton

Unicorn

U p in the sky I saw unicorns, they were cute!

N o scary monsters or unicorns of fairies

I n the clouds I saw a queen unicorn, she was cute

C orn, some unicorns have corns and some do not

O n the ground there were a lot of unicorns but they could fly

R ound in the tree it was a house for fairies

N o monsters, only candy.

Sandija Sanda Andersone (9)
Discovery Primary School, Walton

Dream Land

My dream land is tall and high,
It's hot and cold.
All of the houses are big,
They have lots of rooms.
Lots of Nerf wars every day,
Playing Pokémon outside on the grass.
There's a nice cool wind in the air,
Sunny skies on the beach.
Lots of fun in the garden,
Chocolate fences.
Boxes of pets,
Cats being cute and roaming around.

Bobby Parry (7)
Discovery Primary School, Walton

My Best Dream

As I arrived
It seemed to call my name
Flowers, it seemed to rain.

As I strode further in
I sensed some movement
Then I heard a crack
I looked around.

When I saw a cloud of sparkling dust
Fairy dust in fact
I knew it was a magical place.

Then I walked forward to see
A fairy surrounded by magical unicorns.

Jamie Shadwell (9)
Discovery Primary School, Walton

Spider

S pider, spider what shall I do?

P lay football? Or play with you? People, people, don't be afraid of the spiders, they are friendly to you

I cry lots to spy and lots of pie

D anger, danger ahead, what should I do?

E at, eat your dinner or you become servant or so

R ain, rain, tippity-tap making puddles all around.

Dontay Tyler Jeff Moss (8)
Discovery Primary School, Walton

The Rich Dream!

With Mckenzie, my friend in my dream,
We are owners of Money Land
The land was once just a grass island, not when we
came.
When we came we had a remote control
And the land turned into Money Land.
Everyone was happy and they got cars made of money.
We also got to boss people around
And that's when we became owners of Money Land.
Everyone was happy.

Gvidas Bandza (11)
Discovery Primary School, Walton

Candy Land

Trees growing sweets
House made of treats
Strawberries down the street
Cars made of bars
Windows made of Mars
Chocolate streets for cars

All the things you eat
In my dream I had a tree out of cake
And strawberries in the chocolate sauce lake
I bake a cake that is for the boss
All I need are sweets to come join me.

Andreea Iovita (8)
Discovery Primary School, Walton

My Nightmare

N othing will defeat me ever
I n a smelly, old forest
G oing for a walk in the forest
H e is chasing me to the trees
T he spiky stairs sound in the distance
M y heart is pounding with fright
A t the big snaking trees
R attling from the monkeys spanking the leaves
E normous bushes shaking.

Kye Goulding (10)
Discovery Primary School, Walton

Chicken Nuggets

Once upon a dream
There were chicken nuggets being cooked
Then they came alive, run for your life!
Screams everywhere
Chicken nuggets eating people
Then came police sirens but the police got eaten
Call the chicken kebabs!
Everybody hid until the kebabs arrived
The kebabs kill the chicken nuggets
Then everybody says, 'Hooray!'

Makenzie Owen (10)
Discovery Primary School, Walton

Candyland

C andy around me

A mazed and happy

N ow I eat the candy quickly

D elicious I say

Y um, yum

L ove the candy, and have I go again

A nd then I'm full, my tummy is full of sweets

N ow I can have candy for breakfast and candy for dinner

D essert is candy again!

Deimante Balseryte (10)
Discovery Primary School, Walton

Dragons!

D eath waiting for every animal in any place
R oaring heard from miles away
A dragon waiting for you in every corner
G obbling them all up in his burning mouth
O n bubbling, hot lava you can see bones
N ever enough for that hungry monster
S weet dinner every day, which is only meat.

Ugne Stankute (8)
Discovery Primary School, Walton

Scary Dreams All Around Me

Spiders wiggle and jiggle,
They give me a fright but not as scary
As pirates sailing the seven seas.

Along came the dragons,
Pirates don't fear, the fairies are here
No time to cheer

Raindrops of hearts start to fall
I've had such a ball
It's time to say goodbye to you all
Goodnight.

Maddison Sullivan-Andrews (8)
Discovery Primary School, Walton

Alfie's Poem

I felt happy about living in Dreamland
My house was made out of candy and the trees were candyfloss.
Every time I went outside it was sunny day
And I wanted to play so I went outside
To the mega slides
Then I pressed the button and nothing happened
I pressed it a thousand times and still nothing happened
Then it worked!

Alfie Milton (9)
Discovery Primary School, Walton

I See A Wizard

I see a wizard who is tall and scary
I see a wizard who has a staff and cape
I see a wizard who has a pointed hat and a purple
cloak
He's getting closer and closer until he mutters,
'Hi, my name is Harry Potter.'
He invited me for dinner and I realised
I am the main course.

Connor Knox-Brown (10)
Discovery Primary School, Walton

Father And Daughter

This is my poem, sad but true
It's about my father that I once knew
My family lost him to cancer when I was five
I wasn't ready for him to die
I now see him in my dreams
The best part is when he visits me
I see him step out of a speck of light
That's when he tells me, 'I love you, goodnight!'

Amy-Louise Lonergan (10)
Discovery Primary School, Walton

Unisaur

U ndiscovered places that I see
N aughty dinosaurs looking at me
I live in a house of delicious chocolate
S ugar beaches around the house
A mazing water trees, chocolate lakes
U nisaurs are looking at my face
R ed roses for my BFF, Unisaur!

William Hensby (10) & Joshua Peters
Discovery Primary School, Walton

Time To Die

Once upon a dream
I saw a blood-red beam
Someone said
I found a bed.

Then I heard a bird sing
Night night, what a fright!

I thought I heard a person say
Time to die, goodbye.

I'm tripping and trembling
What to do?
I wake up in my bed
And I am not dead!

Jade Harris (10)
Discovery Primary School, Walton

Fairy Tale Land

F airies carry joy around
A fter joy, happiness will come
I n and out fairies are
R are fairies are important
Y ou are as fragile as a flower
L and on the ground
A nd never leave
N ever ever fly away
D on't die because you belong in Fairyland.

Kearia Blackledge
Discovery Primary School, Walton

The Stars

The stars
The stars
They shine so bright
In the night sky
The sky is so dark
But the stars shine
Like glimmering gold
There are so many
Types of stars
I don't know which one
I like!
Do you know which
One you like?
Now that's a question
You need to think about.

Robyn-Danni Turner (9)
Discovery Primary School, Walton

Football

F ootball prepared on the centre circle
O verreacting once I score
O n my toes waiting to receive
T he ball once and for all
B anging goal by my good friend Thomas
A ll of the team stand in shock
L ater we party and get drunk
L ost the game, oh well!

Jake Forrest (11)
Discovery Primary School, Walton

Dreamland

I dream that I grow up, I'll go to Lithuania, my country
I think I will want to work as a doctor or a teacher
I want to work as a doctor because to me it looks very,
very interesting.
And why I want to be a teacher is because it looks like
fun.
I would have a big house, just for me and I'd be so
happy.

Gintare Ivanauskaite (9)
Discovery Primary School, Walton

My Big Dream

A cting is my big dream
C ircling the backstage floor before a big show
T rying to remember the lines I've learnt
I nside I feel as wobbly as jelly
N ervously, I wait for my auditions
G enerous adults help me out

Remember, believe in yourself!

Grace Barden
Discovery Primary School, Walton

Delightful Dreams

D reams are mysterious and magical

R oughness may happen in a dream, like a big scary monster.

E veryone has dreams. Some are deadly and full of danger!

A nything can happen at all, even a rocket made of monkeys.

M agical creatures you will meet that are good and evil.

Jimmy Hines (8)
Discovery Primary School, Walton

Slenderman

S creaming in the night
L anding light flickering
E mergency escape
N o, do not stay
D o not look back
E ek goes a door
R un for your life
M eet when you can
A sk for help
N ever fight back.

Benjamin Spolander (10)
Discovery Primary School, Walton

A Boy With A Nightmare

I was in a dark corridor
And I saw a door
I opened the door and I saw a boy
He was holding a bowl
The place was familiar.

His blood should be on the floor
The blood was not on the floor but in his bowl
The boy hit me in the head with a hammer.

Mario Valentin Ciortan (9)
Discovery Primary School, Walton

My Nightmares

I felt scared getting crushed
I was terrified
It was a spider that scared me
I was terrified of soldier ants because they bite hands
badly
It scared me so much
The dream was falling off a cliff
It was the scariest thing in my life, falling a thousand
feet.

Dylan Green (9)
Discovery Primary School, Walton

The Countryside Life

Butterflies flap
While others clap
Yellow flowers swish
A buttercup dish
Lays buzzing bees
For they only see
As yellow as can be
Night-time carnivals
Shallow waterfalls
But they're not as bright as the moon's
Night light.

Cai Clapham (11)
Discovery Primary School, Walton

When I Grow Up!

T eacher when I grow up

E veryone will listen to me

A ttention! Attention!

C ake will come to me from my children

H ave lots of fun but never tell the head teacher

E veryone helps everyone

R ight, sit down, off we go.

Bethany Coenen (8)
Discovery Primary School, Walton

Football

F ootball is a great sport

O utstanding goals scored

O oh the crowd cheer

T he ball is collected ready for the match

B rilliant save

A mazing goalkeeper

L ovely dribbling

L oud cheering from the crowd.

Thomas Coenen (11)
Discovery Primary School, Walton

Floating Through The Sky

Floating into the sky following the clouds
Floating like an angel up in the clouds
While floating into the clouds there was singing like a
lovely choir song.

One day a storm hit
The storm was as bad as a bull
The lovely angels, stopped the storm.

Darci Adams (9)
Discovery Primary School, Walton

Dreams

D reams are wonderful you can dream about anything

R eading makes you think about dreams

E verything can work in your dreams

A nything is possible in your dreams

M any things to choose from

S ometimes you can get scary dreams.

Finley Walker (8)
Discovery Primary School, Walton

My Dreams

M e and you may be
Y ou shine as bright as a bee

D ive into a deep pool
R eading is very cool
E very day I miss you
A nd it is true
M um, I miss you
S o why did you have to go so early?

Aiden Groves (9)
Discovery Primary School, Walton

Dream

D og, doctors and dragons
R abbits, rats sailing and running rhinos
E meralds and elephants eating eggs
A pples, animals, arrows and angels
M ummy is magic, monkeys making a mess and motorbikes

Dreams are amazing.

Elena Balaci, Alise, Katie Page, Lavinia & Adriana
Discovery Primary School, Walton

Emerald Secret

U ltima curse

L ove forgot

T emperamental

I magination

M agic emerald

A nything safe

C ure haste

U ntied past

R eal emotions

S oul secret

E yes forbid.

Lily West (11)
Discovery Primary School, Walton

Dinosaur

In the dinosaur land there are lots of dinosaurs
They drink at the river
I can see a view of Dinosaur Land
I see a beautiful dinosaur
I see a builder and a teacher dinosaur
The teacher is going to die
The dinosaur eats lots
Dinosaurs are dying.

Tajus Cicika (9)
Discovery Primary School, Walton

Once Upon A Dream

Once upon a time I miaowed like a cat
Once upon a dream I flew like a bat
Once upon a dream I roared like a lion
Once upon a dream I slithered like a python
However, you must be aware of the grizzly bear
That awaits in your terrifying nightmare!

Isa Hussain (10)
Discovery Primary School, Walton

Dreams

D reams are magical with magic creatures

R iding on every night continuously

E very creature magical and fun

A ll dreams bring heart's desire to everyone

M aybe dragons or unicorns

S ome good and some bad.

Kaitlin Martin (8)

Discovery Primary School, Walton

Dinoroar

D o not mess with these creatures
I also know it
N ever go near these creatures
O r they'll stop and look at you
R ulers of all land
O ver the world
A big pile of mad animals
R oar!

James Murawski (9)
Discovery Primary School, Walton

Funnyland

The trees are full of Lego
where a boy ate some Haribo
He then rowed a boat
whilst wearing a coat
After that, he fed a goat
who had a ring
Which made a ting
Then he said goodbye
But he told a lie
so he went home to cry.

Lucas Ward (7)
Discovery Primary School, Walton

Lego Figures

Lego figures made from multi coloured sand
All these are from Lego Land
Lego figures are the best thing ever but
I would rather like a feather
Lego figures come in all shapes and sizes
They are definitely good surprises.

Oliver Leon Ashley Profitt (8)
Discovery Primary School, Walton

As Empty As A Jar

I felt cold as the snow was falling
The lantern went out
I felt something like I had no soul
I kept going through like there was a light in my heart that said,
'Keep on going you still have time!'
I finally reached my goal!

Nathaniel Slupek (9)
Discovery Primary School, Walton

Cristiano Ronaldo

Mesmerised while watching him play
Hoping to impress the press
People celebrate a great day
he runs to the tunnel but then spots me
The man himself gives me his top
And still to the day with glee.

Colbey James Ring (11)
Discovery Primary School, Walton

The Unihorse In Candy Land

Candy,
Oh a universe,
I wanna ride the unihorse as fast as lightning,
Come on Wiktoria, let's go.
Mmm, so yummy
I want more.
This is such good food.
Wiktoria, isn't it good?
Mmm, let's eat more.

Mariya Owen (10)
Discovery Primary School, Walton

Untitled

I lived in the world sixty-five million years ago
When people had dino pets
I had five raptors, four T-rexes, three spinos
And two allosauruses
My largest T-rex was as big as a mammoth
My raptor was as fast as cheetahs.

Elias Williams (9)
Discovery Primary School, Walton

Abandon Ship!

P irates terrorise the ocean

I feel quite seasick

R ocks are feared by many

A cannonball hits the ship

T he vessel is destroyed

E very hope is lost

S ailors abandon ship.

Niall Grimshaw (11)

Discovery Primary School, Walton

Grand Prix Dream

R ace in the Grand Prix
A rocket whizzes past my head
C ool cars zoom past me
I n England we are famous for sport
N o one can beat our records
G olden trophies get stacked up.

Rhyley James Canham (10)
Discovery Primary School, Walton

Famous

F ancy mansions
A ffordable projects with amazing vehicles
M oney for prize-worthy gifts
O ut of this world
U nicorns flying up and down
S erving chips and ice cream.

Luka Baines-Howley (11)
Discovery Primary School, Walton

Famous

F ancy mansions
A ffordable profits with amazing vehicles
M oney for prize-worthy gifts
O ut of this world
U nicorns exploring above
S eeing us below exploring above.

Rhyannon Moisey-Clarke (10)
Discovery Primary School, Walton

Dragons

D ragons are coming

R onald protects me

A ngrily

G lossy boat across the

O cean of fluffy clouds

N ight is approaching

S torms are coming tonight.

Cassie Faulkner (10)

Discovery Primary School, Walton

Untitled

In my dream
I am a superhero breathing out fire
like a dragon with fiery hot skin.
I throw fireballs out.
I live in a volcano as hot as the sun.
I fly as far as the speed of light.

Umar Mahmud (9)
Discovery Primary School, Walton

Fairies Dancing

Fairies were dancing in the trees
We fell in the trees and cut ourselves
My other fairy friend Maria was with me
I was excited because Maria was with me
The forest was in Sandringham.

Grace Hazel Zajac (11)
Discovery Primary School, Walton

Unicorn

U nicorns jumping around
N ice fur
I s that a unicorn?
C olourful unicorns
O n a field
R oaming around
N ice unicorn.

Melda (10)
Discovery Primary School, Walton

Dreams

D reams are wonderful
R ead then imagine
E verybody should dream
A ll have fun
M agical fun is always there
S mile then dream.

Magda Stanczyk (8)
Discovery Primary School, Walton

Dreams Are Big

D reams are fun
R unning really fast
E verybody likes dreaming
A ll of the world likes dreaming
M y dreams are excellent!

Bismah Hussain (8)
Discovery Primary School, Walton

Dream World

Unicorns fly and eat pie
Guinea pigs spy on things passing by
Once I dreamed I was swimming in jeans and singing
Rats miaow, cats squeak and mice peek!

Isabella Rose Parsons (8)
Discovery Primary School, Walton

Dancer

D ancing on the stage
A mazing moves
N ow performing
C ome see
E ating food
R ipping clothes.

Kaitlin Clark (11)
Discovery Primary School, Walton

Untitled

I live in a wood
Made of sweets
The floor is made of fruit sherbet
The trees are candyfloss
The path is made of golden sprinkles.

Reagan Morson (9)
Discovery Primary School, Walton

Unicorns

U niversal
N ightmares
I ggy
C omes across the
O cean
R unning from
N ightmares.

Holly Christine (11)
Discovery Primary School, Walton

Dreaming

Dreaming unicorns
Playing with fairies
Grow angel wings
Wish on a star
That's my dream
When my PJs dance.

Alice Bettany (8)
Discovery Primary School, Walton

Dream Big

I am the world's best footballer
My name is Brodiey Ring
Everybody happy
Like a dream
Dreams are fun.

Brodiey Jack Ring (8)
Discovery Primary School, Walton

The Day Of Evil

On the wonderful dreamland day
Evil lies ahead ready to pounce on the world
The spider army come out to play
While the unicorns are away on holiday
Unicorns smell evil's rise
From the devil's cave down below
A war has started in this place
OK, this is a scary case!
Spiders rise from the dirt below
Unicorns rush in with a low stampede
War goes on with a bang and a *crash!*
Unicorns lash out their horns
Ready to fight on this dark, dark night
Hooray! Hooray! The war has topped
Stopped with a bang, crash and a pop
All is well so here I go
I wake up but now I see
On the lawn lays a mythical rainbow horn.

Sophia Maderbocus (9)
Elm Road Primary School, Wisbech

Albert Einstein's New Invention

I made an invention
That I showed at a sci-fi convention
My cranky peculiar invention
Bought a lot of attention

I made a potion
That was bubbling like a fish
It made a bang
So I got an important promotion

I was very delighted
Because of something that I saw
A weird-shaped cloud dancing then popping like
popcorn
I was so, so bored
Then I saw Sir Isaac Newton
Who was born in Lincoln
He discovered the staggering force of gravity
But could not stop getting hit on the head with an
apple.

Callum Malkin (10)
Elm Road Primary School, Wisbech

Boo

I am in an office, sitting there feeling tedious
And I prefer a stuffing
An object is staring like it's no bother
I then scream like no other
Then it pounces on me and bites me on the neck
It turns into dust like spice falling
I'm infected, what will I do?
I see a syringe out of the hole but will I make it?
I reach it, but I'm feeling evil
I got there, I get the syringe and poke it into me
I feel better
I go home, I am happy and I sleep for three days
What a dream!

Kastytis Dambrauskas (9)
Elm Road Primary School, Wisbech

My Sweet Dreams

When I got to sleep I dream of treats
Jelly tots and ice cream pots
I dream of Angel Delight
I could eat all night
Jam roly-poly with custard galore, mmm
That's my favourite that I adore
With apple pie I'm never too shy
Meringue nests are simply the best
With lots of cream, you know what I mean
Ice cream sundae even on a Monday
Oh strawberries and cream
My dream is lovely
As a fairy tale can be.

Alina Skok (10)
Elm Road Primary School, Wisbech

The Football Bros

I'm stuck in a dream with my big bro
In a very big house
With slates that are rapping 'yos'
And we have a pet mouse
A mini football pitch in our back yard
Where me and my bro play
And I'd like to say
On a team, we are rock hard
As our plants stand up tall
We buy season tickets
When we get back we hear the birds call
We see a bottle then my bro says, 'Flip it!'
I land it.

Henry Plume (10)
Elm Road Primary School, Wisbech

War Robot!

I live in Tokyo
With a giant war machine
Outside my house on my driveway and kerb!
With my black Lamborghini poised to strike
All powered up and ready to attack
Controlled with an Xbox IS
Connected to a Lamborghini
He's in war all locked and loaded
One dinobot goes *kaboom*, another gets chopped in
half
Ssh!
Out comes a sword from Lambona's hand
Out comes another from the other!

Henry Hussick (9)
Elm Road Primary School, Wisbech

Naughty Nightmares

Nightmares are scary things
They normally come with bites or stings
You always get stuck in frightening dreams
They normally end with lightning or screams
Have you ever been chased in a dream?
After all of the screams, you end up weak
You can never speak
When you've had a bad shriek
Your eyes start to leak
As the deathly people come out to play
I wake up to the start of a new day.

Ruben Hughes (9)
Elm Road Primary School, Wisbech

Weather

Oh I wish, oh I wish
That the grass would be green
And the pink flowers would lean just like swans
Up to the bright blue sky
And would not spy
That the trees would look wonderful
And the plants would dance happily
O how I love the land
And the smooth sand
Always goes swish
That tickles your feet with laughter
O I wish, o I wish
That the world would be amazing.

Emilija Stonkute (10)
Elm Road Primary School, Wisbech

The Magical Land Of Fairies

Once in a dream there was a fairy
Who shown me a land that no one's ever seen.
She said I'd appear with a magical bang
And there I was in the magical land!
All I could see was a beautiful castle
With a wonderful and bright garden,
And all I could hear was the howling wind
And a barking dog.
But there in the corner of my eye
There was a fairy zooming by!

Emili Siskaite (10)
Elm Road Primary School, Wisbech

Where Am I Going?

I could see a boat without an owner
the waves were as still as a statue
I step in and the first thing I saw was a unicorn
I wonder why there was on, but that did not matter
I hopped on it's back and somehow she gave me a flower
After a while, I was a bit itchy so I decided to look down
When I looked down I realised
I was wearing a cartoon outfit with bats.

Bianca Martins (9)
Elm Road Primary School, Wisbech

My Mermaid Dreams

When I got to sleep I dream of mermaids
With colourful tails and swooshing hair
I dream of pearls
I could play with all night
Giant castles full of treats, *mmm*
Mermaids laying on the sand
Dancing fish with multicoloured scales
The sunlight is going down
Bedtime now
How lovely could a dream be
With all these beautiful things!

Patrycja Snopek (9)
Elm Road Primary School, Wisbech

Mythical Mystery

The sky is a galaxy with fluffy, candyfloss clouds
The grass is as turquoise as a butterfly
These flowers are as beautiful as Mrs Carter
The creatures are as small as a ladybug
Oh, look it's a girl
She's coming through the sky!
Oh, wait she's gone
She must be from another world
But she's gone through to the dark realm.

Sadia Ahmed (8)
Elm Road Primary School, Wisbech

Funny Football

Footballers bouncing in the mud
Not caring about popping the ball with their studs
Archie kicks Messi out of the team
Getting a new kit that was green
Out of the team goes Neymar Jr
Making him feel a bit peculiar

Archie fools four defenders
Then back heels it to me
Then I shoot with a Ribona
It goes twiddly diddly dee.

Justin Woods (9)
Elm Road Primary School, Wisbech

Magical Moments

Oh I hope, oh I hope
One day I will find the land of magic
Where the trees swish and wish like a genie
Where the bright sun spies in the sky
Oh I hope, oh I hope
One day I will find the land of magic
Where the creatures roam and the rivers flow,
Where the mythical creatures walk

Here and there.

Amelia Godfrey (10)
Elm Road Primary School, Wisbech

I Had A Dream

I had a dream about a friend
His name is Jack
He smelt like cookies
he has a deadly back
He helped me do work and my flying moonwalk
To show to creatures
He lived in Tokyo
The capital of Japan
He made me fly over the world
And made me king
Then I showed my bling.

Edward Griffin Murrell (8)
Elm Road Primary School, Wisbech

Vampire Spider

In the middle of nowhere
I saw a vampire spider!
The big hairy spider walked up me,
And bit me,
Who or what will it bite next?
I am frozen with fear!
The spider's venom started to turn me into a spider.
Agony as four more arms grow out of my body.

Jenna-Marie Adams (8)
Elm Road Primary School, Wisbech

What's Your Wish?

I worry where I am
What animal am I?
This makes me think
I think I am a unicorn
Hooray! I'm a unicorn
I have a golden horn
A beautiful horn
A beautiful, sparkly mane!
For a job
I grant wishes
What is your wish?

Leona Hobbs (8)
Elm Road Primary School, Wisbech

Dreams

D ancing and prancing
R unning and screaming happily
E ating over foot long chocolate houses
A nd seeing flying giraffes pass by
M oney grows from trees in my dreams
S ee your dreams come to life.

Amanda Mazure (10)
Elm Road Primary School, Wisbech

My World

I'm in a Roblox world
No way to escape
No one wants to be friends with me
Because of my skin
I tried everything
But it didn't work
So I played a different game
Called Angry Birds
And I've completed it.

Alex Maniyathattu Binu (9)
Elm Road Primary School, Wisbech

Who Bit Who

I'm on the pitch and who do I see?
Dracula and Suárez
Both baring teeth
They stare!
They glare!
At each other, then at me
As quick as a flash
I flee!

Archie Wiles (8)
Elm Road Primary School, Wisbech

Once Upon A Dream

As the carriage sped up, we left Earth
We reached Mars and the red rocks glistened in the
sun
Then we got to the sun
We went inside, it was as hot as fire
My lizard was petrified
And couldn't shut its mouth like a statue
I heard a whoosh as a rocket passed us
It was a while as a cloud on a summer's day
The rocket was sprinting away from Earth
Next was Saturn, it was as if it was hula-hooping
The dust was glistening like glitter
Saturn's planet looked like red rocky road
So tasty and scrumptious
Our travelling was over
It was like waking up from a dream
Forgetting everything, as bad as the dark.

Lauren Cove (11)
Kimbolton Preparatory School, Huntingdon

Wonderland

Fish fly, dance then jump into the blue wasteland
Giants jump and thump to make a storm
It rains wine and hails gumballs as I spread my arms to gaze
Seven dwarfs mine away for boiled sweets
While princesses skateboard down the rocky road hill
Mermaids lap and swirl like ribbons in the air, then jump into the blue
Crimson takes over the lace sky
And fairies leap with spirits through the rainbow.

Sammy-Jo Webb (11)
Kimbolton Preparatory School, Huntingdon

My Dream Getting Lost

G inger my hamster as boring as ever
E ven in the freezing weather
T issues I need, I've caught a cold
T elephone rings, but I'm brave and bold
I go outside not scared at all
N ot allowed to pass the big wall
G etting scared, 'No I'm not.'

L ots of shadows, but I'm not a tiny tot
O ver the big hill
S o many trees, no sign of my mill
T rees surround me, I'm in a nightmare but most of all
I'm lost.

Louise Lodge (8)
Kirkstone House School, Baston

The Ghost, The Bat And The Cat

The ghost is under your seat
Scared you must be
Because of its nasty tricks
It is called Bob the bat
The bat is black
It's very fat
The vampires bat
The vampires bat sucks your blood
Witch
Witch on a broomstick
I ran for my life
Tomb in my way
Clambered on top of it
Hot and sweaty I carried on
The cat is black
It lives in a barn
It was very scary
Mrs Fallowfield went down it.

Honor Pearson (9)
Kirkstone House School, Baston

Dream Haikus

Sky blue so shiny
The navy blue so happy
Blue so glistening

Playing with a bone
A golden cocker spaniel
So cute and fluffy

The school with no boys
With lots of sport and fixtures
Lots of art and fun.

Isabella Anstee (10)
Kirkstone House School, Baston

In My Future Dream

In my future dream
I fly high in the sky
In my future dream
I fly so so high
In my future dream
I live an endless life of luxury
And super cool machines
Handed to me
On a golden plate.

Matteo Tamer Sadek (11)
Kirkstone House School, Baston

Deep, Dark Things

In the deep dark night
In the deep dark forest
In the deep dark hole in the tree
There was a deep dark bear
With deep dark fur
Who was much more angry than me.

In his deep dark eyes
I saw deep dark twinkles
Like the green of the evergreen tree.

In my deep dark brain
I thought deep dark thoughts
And I pushed back through the tickly leaves.

Suddenly, I woke up
Finding I was stroking
Something furry by my knee.

Fancy that!
It was just a dream about my cat.

Tilda Fox Holland (8)
Milton Road Primary School, Cambridge

Snow Monsters

Is it day or is it night?
Is it land or in the sky?
Everything around me is white with ice
When snowy monsters with fiery eyes

Come to me nearer and nearer
Till I am paralysed with fear!
I don't know what they want from me
Their hideous faces are all I can see.

I feel like screaming and shouting for help
But nothing comes out not even a yelp
They are pouncing at me and, 'Oh dear!'
When, 'Wake up darling,' Mum's voice I hear.

Petar Cucakovic (8)
Milton Road Primary School, Cambridge

Danger

I'm in a room of darkness
Stranded all by myself
With only the comfort of predators
Lurking on the shelf
They look like toys but I believe
That one day they'll come true
There are a lion, a cheetah and another one
I don't know who
So now I'm warning you
If you awake
In a room of darkness
Please be careful
I can't tell you what happened
When I made one mistake.

Maeve Talulla Shankar (8)
Milton Road Primary School, Cambridge

Christmas

C ambridge and most of the world celebrate
H appiest day of the year I say
R hythm flows through the songs
I ndeed children stay up too long
S ometimes it snows sometimes it doesn't
T ime to meet family and cousins
M erry Christmas everyone
A fter all the work was done
S o what will you have Christmas Day?

William Wratten
Milton Road Primary School, Cambridge

The River

The river is blue
And it might be next to you
It can't be high in the sky
It can only be low as the level of your big toe
The river can be in a line which is fine
When the river is mean
You can't leave and watch a scene
The river enemy is dams
which makes him swirl and slam
It makes him dirty
The dam's called Berty.

Loïc River Comment (9)
Milton Road Primary School, Cambridge

Pixies Flying

P ixies flying through the night
I nside I feel super bright
X ylophone music drifts through the air
I tching closer to a pixie fair
E very pixie's fast asleep
S o bright lights shine on everyone.

Genevieve White (8)
Milton Road Primary School, Cambridge

Easter

E aster is a time for fun
A mazing things can happen
S ee the Easter bunny hopping by
T urn your mind to aim high
E aster is nearly over
R eady to have some Easter buns.

Isobel Mann (8)
Milton Road Primary School, Cambridge

The River

The river's a monster
It takes all your stuff
The river is a monster
He's kind but a bit rough
The river is so strong
It takes all your stuff
The river is so nice
But it still flings.

Jassim Laoukili (9)
Milton Road Primary School, Cambridge

Nightmares

N ightmares are scary, what will happen this time?

I guanadons are chasing me around a dark forest

G one are the dinosaurs, but who knows what's round the corner

H ow can this be, there are monsters?

T yrannosaurus rex is surely enough

M onsters have returned all around the forest

A friendly wizard comes

R oars are heard from my left so I head right

E ast is where I'm heading hopefully to safety

S cared as can be, soon it's morning.

Krishnan Thillai (8)
University Of Cambridge Primary School, Cambridge

Moon Whispered

Moon whispered
In the shadows of the stars
The moon's surface crisps
when the sun is hottest
The moon rays run through space

The planets sing and dance
The dwarf planet freezes like freezers, because they are far away
The milky way glows colourfully
When the light has passed
Happily the galaxy slumbers
When it is night.

Monty Chatfield (8)
University Of Cambridge Primary School, Cambridge

Stars Shine

Stars make shimmering light to create a calming
beautiful night
The stars do everything right and the moon has all the
might
When the sun starts to set and calmly
the wind blows the stars start to smile
And the sun is one billion miles
when the children are getting fed, the sun is in its bed.

Vanya Ethan Fromant Skjodt (8)
University Of Cambridge Primary School, Cambridge

Clouds Whisper

Clouds whisper
While walking
In the moonlight

Clouds talk
In the darkness
Of the night

Clouds shout
While singing
In the loudness of the sun

Clouds scream
In choirs
Instead of singing alone.

Thomas Harrison-Zeronis (8)
University Of Cambridge Primary School, Cambridge

The Groaning Street

The traffic groaned
In the tarmac night
When the bins started to bite
The street lamps snarled
The roaring wind started to fight
When the shops slept with desperate delight
The cars filled up with fear
When the deserted night slept.

Freddie Chatfield (8)
University Of Cambridge Primary School, Cambridge

The Forest

In the forest
The trees dance in the glimmering moonlight
As the flaming eye of the sun rose in the sky
The moonlight fell into a pit and the sun shone
Soon the moon will fly into the sky again
As if to say, 'I'm high in the sky!'

Willoughby Jones (8)
University Of Cambridge Primary School, Cambridge

River Night

The moon started to open, its sparkly shimmering eye
at the rotting river
Horrible heat like a book, all about desert's heat
crossing a storm
Slowing down the magical moon.

Isabella Wilkes-Read (8)
University Of Cambridge Primary School, Cambridge

Shadows Drink The Sun

Shadows as black as deep space
Advance on the magnificent yellow sun
Covering them up
The shadows drink in the sun
Like indestructible unstoppable black shapes.

Alec Longden (8)
University Of Cambridge Primary School, Cambridge

The Dancing Unicorn

The dancing unicorn's horn sparkled in the moonlight,
I was speechless
The sparkles burned my skin slightly
As the unicorn tapped its hooves
It flew away.

Alice Halsey (8)
University Of Cambridge Primary School, Cambridge

Midnight Mummy

When I was walking down the street - it was the middle of the night,
Then I suddenly heard a shriek and I got quite a fright.
I ran around like a headless chicken wondering what to do,
It was then that I decided I must leave: I must go.

I ran around the playground, and screamed out loud in fear,
I had to escape the mummy that was cursed in ancient years.
I couldn't think of anything, my heart was beating too fast,
I didn't want to be caught by the evil from the past.

I quickly sprinted to school, and hid inside a classroom;
When I saw the mummified ghoul, I thought it had escaped its tomb.
The mummy stretched out its wrapped-up arms and loudly growled at me,
But luckily I heard my alarm that woke me from my dream.

Tristan Hicks (11)
West Walton Community Primary School, West Walton

This Was An Interesting Day

Just as we pulled up at the famous zoo,
I jumped out the car with so much excitement
And looked around as an elephant flew
I knew this was going to be an interesting day.

We walked past the demon stingrays.
They stared at us deadly as we kept on walking by.
We overheard people talking about what had
happened on previous days,
I knew this was going to be an interesting day.

The day seemed normal to start off,
Until that moment shock startled me.
Everyone started to cough,
I knew this was going to be a strange day.

Dust flew up in people's faces,
I could hear my brain telling me to get out - but I didn't
listen.
All the animals were loose and people were running
and tripping over their shoelaces,
I knew this was going to be an interesting day.

The animals at the zoo were let loose,
The poor people who worked there didn't know what to do!
The sound of bare feet trotted over the hard concrete followed by a loud screeching goose,
I didn't see what was coming next.

It sounded like a band gone wrong as the crew of animals ran off down the main road!
No one knew where they were going so they got in their cars and followed.
I was so intrigued at this point I wanted to follow the car load,
I didn't know what was going on but I wanted to find out.

The animals were heading for Buckingham Palace; what was going on?
I thought to myself how excited I was to see what was going to happen.
The animals were off: they were gone,
The criminal animals went in the palace, I saw them with my eyes as they grew.

We waited a few minutes as the crime was to be seen,
But the animals came out looking proud of themselves.
Police and guards chased them out and pointed them
to where they had just been,
In the escapists' hands the crowds saw the most
beloved crown jewels.

That was the most exciting day out I've been on,
I thought to myself,
Before I found out I've been living in dream land for the
past eight hours.

Holly Walker (11)
West Walton Community Primary School, West Walton

Once Upon A Dream

S he'd just finished her amazing jazz practise,

W hen she went outside, she rose straight into the pale blue sky

E mily saw a wonderful place, dark and twinkly, space

E mily saw two of her bright furry friends which are monsters.

T hey floated around happily in extraordinary space

D ancing, Emily started growing magical powers

R ising more into the air they decided to go to Emily's extravagant house

E legant and beautiful, it was also glittery with lots of shades of purple, blue and red.

A mazingly, they saw two beautiful unicorns with rainbow manes at the front of her house

M orning came and her mum started waking Emily and she forgot all about the sweet dream.

S he never remembered the dream ever again.

Lorin Sahin (11)
West Walton Community Primary School, West Walton

Once Upon A Nightmare

Since I have circled into the forest,
My cats and I,
All I can identify is a small cottage,
I'm going to cry!

It had a rusty broken door,
Falling off the roof with the crash of metal -
Are tiles,
It hit a flower, now it's lost a petal.

A man was rummaging near the door,
Then a window smashed with a pause.
He was looking through a hole in the floor,
Then he came out. What was the cause?

A little plump man,
With an angry expression!
He came closer,
I looked down in depression.

He pulled a rusty wooden pipe from his pocket
We're no longer in the forest!
We have teleported!
Then I heard someone call out, 'Forist.'

It was a snake-like figure,
He was saying hi.
Then a lady with frizzed hair,
She waved to come by.

The man followed her,
His pruned curled fingers round my shoulder.
He took me with him,
I was getting colder.

I put the cats in their cat-pack,
So the man couldn't take them away.
We went in the mansion,
And there sat a snake, I backed away.

He talked in a snaky language,
'Bla bla bla,' he said.
He took me to a dungeon - I think I need a bandage,
And threw me on a stone bed.

Then one of the cats scratched me,
It jumped up.
On the windowsill
There was a barking of a pup.

We ran back to the forest,
Then we got lost.
Then I heard 'Forist',
What will be the cost?

I tried to get up,
But they caught up to me.
They took me to the dungeon,
No escape this time you see.

I saw a little girl,
She unlocked the door.
The door opened wide!
Thanks, little girl from the other side

I went home with her,
But it was a trick!
I tried to escape,
But she turned me into brick.

I screamed then suddenly,
I heard a piercing alarm again.
This time I noticed,
It was my alarm clock.

Keira Evans (11)
West Walton Community Primary School, West Walton

Unicorn Dreaming

U nicorns are walking on lovely rainbows,
N ow I am their magical protector,
I n Unicorn Land it is magical fun,
C ome and join with everyone,
O r you can't come again,
R un away from the evil queen's minions,
N ow come and taste the multicoloured millions.

D ream and dream and never stop,
R unning with the enchanted unicorns is fun,
E at on rainbows like the unicorns do,
A nd you will not want to leave ever again,
M y unicorn friends won't ever hurt you,
I f you don't ever hurt them,
N ow it is time for me to go,
G o and return again tomorrow.

Keira Lawrence (11)
West Walton Community Primary School, West Walton

Once Upon A Nightmare

I am gliding through space,
Looking at the endless void around me.
All I can identify is the beautiful stars.
Oh the magical things I can see!

I have another look around,
And then I can see,
An exciting island -
Right behind me!

I examine the island,
With lots of hope,
And then I can see it,
A majestic dragon - but he is caught in a rope.

I dive towards the island,
Hoping I can save him,
His colours flashing through the rainbow,
I think I will name him Tim.

Who captured him?
Is he OK?
I hope I can untie him,
So he can fly away.

I have now reached the island
And I have a look around,
Then an evil-grinning clown comes towards me,
Making absolutely no sound...

I run as fast as I can,
Trying to escape,
But the next thing I know,
I am stuck in tape.

He puts me with the dragon,
Leaving us to die,
I am screaming and kicking about,
I think I am going to cry.

But suddenly the dragon,
Made a sudden roar,
And burnt all the rope down,
He is flying for the door.

Unfortunately I am still stuck,
So the dragon turned around,
He burnt all the tape away,
And I ran round and round.

He's so happy;
So am I,
I am dancing around in happiness,

I think I am going to cry...
But now the time has come,
Where I must go back home,
The dragon goes to his homeland,
And I am all alone.

Since I have arrived in this universe,
I have had a lot of fun.
But now it is the end of my adventure,
And I wake up being blinded by the sun.

Evie Lane (11)
West Walton Community Primary School, West Walton

Mr Spider Nightmare!

As I go to sleep tonight
I feel as if a nightmare is here.
I'm surrounded by fear and fright
And all I see is my deepest enemy - Mr Spider!

How dare he appear in my dream?
With his long black legs and hairy head.
Too bad I don't have a laser beam,
Or I would zap this horrifying creature off the scene!

And then with a stroke of luck,
My mum shouted, 'Get up!'
Turns out that my alarm is broken...
But at least I have finally been awoken.

Now let's forget about this horrible dream
And continue the day spider-free!

Sonny Lee Sandberg (11)
West Walton Community Primary School, West Walton

My Ballet Dream

As I stepped outside,
My whole body was filled with pride.
I slowly prepared myself by the sunset,
As my mind was set to become Odette.

I began to dance with all my heart,
As I wish I could go to the Paris School of Arts.
Soon I realise darkness has controlled the sky,
My mind and heart began to cry.

I go to bed to begin my night,
That will be filled with wonder and no fright.
I immediately see the tall tower with a peak so high,
As I watch the grey pigeons fly.

I see something similar to the School of Arts,
When suddenly my life has all become one part.
I start running towards the masterpiece,
Where dancers dance to songs of harmony and peace.

I immediately knew my dreams were bigger,
I thought I could become the ballet figure.
I wish I could know if this was real or not,
The streets were cold; the opposite of hot.

As I walk through the door,
I am determined to dance even more.
I look down realising I am wearing a dress of beauty
and grace,
Knowing this is my new favourite place.

I am wearing a pearly white pair of ballet shoes,
Telling myself I have nothing to lose.
One dance would never hurt,
So I step onto the floor that had not one speck of dirt.

I began to twirl and dance with passion and happiness,
As my world takes away all of my sadness.
I feel I am dancing on a lake.
When I suddenly realise I am now awake.

Olivia Grace Reynolds (11)
West Walton Community Primary School, West Walton

Once Upon A Dream ~ My Nightmare World

Midnight-coloured black vines,
Swirl around me in lines.
My dreamcatcher isn't working,
So it isn't me who is smirking.

They're taking me to an abyss of eternal dark,
Where there is no fun not even a park.
There is, however, all of my fears,
From all of my eventful years.

The vines pull me to the eerie-looking glass,
They push me in so I have to pass.
I go through the glass and experience a
transformation,
I've just crossed into the parallel nightmare dimension.

All of my greatest fears are here,
And some are coming very near.
The vines leave me with a blunt dagger,
So I can scarcely defend myself even from the nagger.

It starts to rain blood so I run to find shelter,
I run quickly under the bone-made helter-skelter.

Unluckily there I find the living dead,
Much to my dread.

I stab every zombie until they shrivel up in pain,
The blood stains on my T-shirt are not in vain.
I know that I'm stuck here until I wake,
Or until my sister gives me a shake.

The blood rain stops and the sun comes in,
I must be rousing so I can put this dream in my
memory bin.
My fears cower and disappear,
As my bedroom starts to reappear.

Isabella Perks (11)
West Walton Community Primary School, West Walton

The Pirate Queen Dream

I have finished my day
And I crawl under the bedsheets,
Ready for the deep sleep...

As I rise from my bed, I remember one word: voyage.
I dress and wake my baby monkey Nana,
Then walk out onto the sunny beach of Miami.
I am met by a crowd of people, waiting for me, their
pirate queen, to step onto the flying ship and take to
the skies.

I watch as the ship descends to the ground
And lowers the gang plank for me,
Which hits the ground, without a sound
And the fiddler plays a song about the sea.

I find myself waving to the people below
While the gangplank is being raised,
My mind racing with excitement and fear,
For I do not know what will happen.

The crew hurry around getting the ship ready to take
off,
It's all rather exciting,
I am shown to my room, where I shall be staying;
There is even a bed for Nana!

Laid out on my bed
Is my cutlass and case.
I walk out onto the deck ready to dine,
But...

On the way to the dining room,
I am struck by a lightning bolt;
There was no pain but I did gain,
Extraordinary superpowers!

Evie Doughty (11)
West Walton Community Primary School, West Walton

Candy Land Dream

I fell asleep in my peaceful, purple bed,
So I could rest my sleepy head,
I fell into a starry galaxy swirl,
Then I began to spin and whirl.

I landed in a delicious candy house,
But all I could see was a giant statue of a chocolate mouse.
I then noticed the stripy candy cane walls,
I saw outside there were salted caramel pools.

The doors were made from rock-hard toffee
And the windows created from clear, thin coffee.
There was a cute ginger cat with tiny blue wings,
And next to it was a dog with lots of pretty rings.

I saw a huge mirror so I took a quick glance,
I was a sweet fairy looking ready to dance.
I had bright, colourful, rainbow hair,
It was wavy, very long and fair.

Then the toffee door opened and three girls walked in
One of them had a stunning fish fin.
One was flying with a lilac mermaid tail,
The other was carrying a lot of important mail

We went and jumped into the pool
But I fell down and down the galaxy hall,
Then I awoke in my snug, cosy bed,
And all I wanted was to be fed.

Emmie May Parker (11)
West Walton Community Primary School, West Walton

Nightmare About To Happen!

Whilst I was sleeping in my bed,
I suddenly woke and thought about dread.

I immediately sat up straight,
Because this time it gave me a fright.

Once I was outside my bones began to shiver,
And I heard Daisy miaow a loud quiver.

I walked slowly right until I got to the park,
Where it was pitch-black dark.

Small silent feet turned into misery,
Because a clown rose from the corner as it said, 'We meet.'

Daisy and I just stopped and stared,
Whilst the clown just glared.

It looked me in the eye suspiciously,
And decided to charge at Daisy and me.

The clown was really quick,
Daisy and I were waiting for the trick.

The clown followed us,
Whilst Daisy and I took the bus.

When we arrived at home we immediately fell asleep
again
And said, 'I am so glad that it was a dream.'

Alfie Kierman (11)
West Walton Community Primary School, West Walton

Wake Up!

I appeared in a dark room,
I looked around, no window, no door.
All I wanted was to leave, soon,
When I looked again, I saw...

There was a shadow in the dark,
It, I could barely see.
On the wall, a deep claw mark,
A feeling approached; it was looking at me.

I thought to myself this was a dream,
But then my heart rate rose.
A dream: it would not seem,
Where was I? I didn't know.

It stood up at seventeen feet,
And put its spiny hand on my shoulder.
Its hand was charcoal, and tied me to a seat,
My blood ran even colder.

My mind was in distress,
The panic lingers.
Was I about to be stabbed through the chest?
Suddenly, I felt its needle fingers.

The needles enveloped my head,
I was scared and when I spoke I did say.
And I suddenly appeared in my bed,
No monster, not today.

Anderson MacCormick (11)
West Walton Community Primary School, West Walton

Once Upon A Dream

I slipped up and fell in a bush,
Fell into a portal, got a little push.
I didn't know who did it
I couldn't guess at all, not a bit.
I carried on walking before I saw a sign,
It said *Welcome To Mars*, that didn't make me feel fine.
I looked behind me to see if there was a portal, it wasn't there,
But there was a bear!
It chased and chased me until I had to stop,
Luckily for me, it just went *pop*.
I woke up in such a shock,
Noticing it was the bear that gave me a little knock.

William Bates (10)
West Walton Community Primary School, West Walton

The Ballerina Confusion

Sitting in my luxury chair,
A beautiful dancer appears at a glance.
She is so breathtaking I can't help but stare.
Mid-arabesque in the blink of an eye
She falls flat on her face,
I hope she doesn't cry!
I'm lying on the floor
Am I the ballerina?
I'm really not sure.
I feel a pain in my leg
What - excuse me, will you say that once more?
Please someone, help me I beg!
I can't hear a thing, everything's turning green
Wake up, time for school,
Was that a dream?
Phew, what a relief!

Phebe Helen Goose (11)
West Walton Community Primary School, West Walton

Nightmare

N ightmares are terrible and are very creepy.

I normally see the creepy clown Ronald McDonald.

G reat giant spooky spiders are scaring me and so is the clown!

H igh up in the sky I see the McDonald copter!

T he soul-like ghost has appeared in front of my bed!

M y bed is now high above the clouds!

A flying zombie flew overhead!

R onald McDonald pushed me off my bed!

E ventually I found myself back in bed at 6am.

Lewis Taylor (11)
West Walton Community Primary School, West Walton

Chicken Nightmare!

I was going on a trip
In my favourite rocket ship
When I crashed into a giant chicken hutch,
In my hand my sword I clutched
I swiped at the chicken
The chicken swiped back.
Then I shouted full-on attack!
The cuts affected me
Then I knew what was key.
The chicken had a scar
So I charged at his scar
Then the chicken ran far.
There I found that I was safe and sound
Lying there in my comforting bed...

'William! Get ready for school!'

William Paul Hanslip (10)
West Walton Community Primary School, West Walton

The Magic Mirror

The magic mirror was there,
So I gave it a gleaming stare.
I saw I was bright green,
Like a long runner bean.
I had a large spiky tail,
And I was as slimy as a snail.
I looked again to see I was light blue,
Like a ball of bubblegum all sticky as glue.
I just wanted to be back to my normal self,
But then I turned into a miniature red elf.
Then I woke up to see,
I was a normal kiddy.
So I went back to my lovely bed,
Because I was a very sleepyhead.

George Buster Moore (11)
West Walton Community Primary School, West Walton

My Nightmare

My mum said I had to go to bed
So I fell into a deep sleep.
Then all of a sudden I saw black, it must be a bad
dream, 'Hello!' shouted the monster.
The monster spoke to me!
Come into the light? 'No, it's too bright!'
But I saw a little red nose, so I hid under my bed
clothes.
I tossed and I turned, I didn't want to see a big clown
staring at me...

Lily Louise Gowler (10)
West Walton Community Primary School, West Walton

Floating Dream

D reaming is lovely

R eading stories every day

E ating vanilla icing from my garden

A re the butterflies dreaming too?

M y house is made from chocolate cake

L oved by many people, young and old

A stonishing results from the crowd

N one hated my house

D id all the animals dream too, I wonder?

Darcey-Mae Jones (11)

West Walton Community Primary School, West Walton

Once Upon A Dream

D ream big like the wings of a unicorn,
R eaching for the stars high up in the sky!
E ating lots of rainbows,
A cting big and strong,
M idnight is coming.

W hat will this bring?
O ut come the stars,
R aining big and loud,
L ighting up the sky,
D id the unicorns fly?

Paige Markham (11)
West Walton Community Primary School, West Walton

Once Upon A Dream

N ight is where the magic happens.

I t is where some scary things happen.

G ot to hide from the monsters.

H urry and try to get out

T hey run faster than you in nightmares.

M ay you find a place to hide.

A way from the monsters.

R un for your life.

E veryone hiding from view.

Tristan Welby (11)

West Walton Community Primary School, West Walton

Holiday Trip

Holiday going
Hotel staying
Floorboards creaking
Food cooking
Mouth eating
Park arriving
Self-losing
Children gasping
Moon glowing
Stars twinkling
Parents worrying
Trees swaying
Leaves rustling
Stranger kidnapping
Children screaming
Parents calling
Stranger running
Children crying.

Shannon Harrison-Wiles (11)
West Walton Community Primary School, West Walton

A Beach Dream

Waves crashing,
Rock smashing,
Children crying,
Sea-fern dying,
Fishnets breaking,
Swim-legs aching,
Beach-ball bobbing,
Heart throbbing,
Ice cream selling,
Mums sunbathing,
Seagulls flying,
Jellyfish stinging,
Arm swelling,
Hospital heading,
Painless awakening.

Morgan Kirk (11)
West Walton Community Primary School, West Walton

Magic

M agic is extremely fun
A piece of magic can do a lot
G reat fun you can have with a pinch of magic
I love to play with magic, I am sure you do too
C ome my friend have some fun

D og or human you can still have fun
R eal life is not a dream
E ggs are just a thing
A bit of love magic has a secret
M agic dreams are the best

W inning can be fun
O ne piece of magic
R elaxing in magic while I sleep
L ying in my bed
D on't you just love magic?

Olivia May Huggett (8)
Wisbech St Mary CE (VA) Primary School, St Mary

The Pirate's Treasure

We were sailing across the ocean
The sea was reflecting the sky
We were all full of emotion
And we all wondered why.

The moon was shining
As bright as the stars
Most of my brothers were laughing
Because they all love Mars.

As the waves were lapping
We all had some fun
Then we started napping
And up came the sun.

The next night we sailed again
That very night we found a den
that actually might have treasure in
How about a number, let's say ten.

Lillie Bardsley (9)
Wisbech St Mary CE (VA) Primary School, St Mary

Nightmare Land

In Nightmare Land there was nowhere to go,
We run very slow.
When monsters chase you there's no point in running,
because it's a marathon long.
It used to be fun and now it is glum.
I wish I could leave but I'm stuck in a spider's web,
And I'm going to be dead.
It isn't fair, children are meant to dream of cats and
dogs,
But I have nightmares of devils and ghosts.
It just isn't fair!

Blake Bevan-Black (9)
Wisbech St Mary CE (VA) Primary School, St Mary

Candy Land!

This strange candy land with bubblegum grass is my
dream land
The clouds taste like cotton candy
With a touch of chewing gum in the middle
I travel through on my gingerbread bus
In my dreams, I don't make a fuss
When I'm asleep my mouth goes *pop*
I never want this feeling to ever stop
The trees are like lollies, their leaves are like fearsome
dolls
I love to dream of Candy Land.

Kezia Sutherill (8)
Wisbech St Mary CE (VA) Primary School, St Mary

Popcorn World

Popcorn World is as fun as a fair
But people never ever want to share
They keep their toys and hide their popcorn
You go near them, they blow their horn
But there's one thing you'll like, candy
You need to look out for Andy!
He eats all the candy in one big bite
Every day people take out their kites
You may go out every day
But you should be careful, I should say.

Ashton Freddie Clarke (8)
Wisbech St Mary CE (VA) Primary School, St Mary

Pokémonland

My dream is Pikachu, Pikachu, a very hungry Pikachu
Raichu, Raichu, a very sleepy Raichu
Pichu, Pichu, a very cute Pichu
Charmander, Charmander, a very silly Charmander
Eevee, Eevee, a very funny Eevee
Flareon, Flareon, a very scary Flareon
Zygard, Zygard, a very scaly Zygard
Zapdos, Zapdos, a flappy Zapdos
Mew, Mew, a happy Mew.

Joshua Abrams-Stebbings (9)
Wisbech St Mary CE (VA) Primary School, St Mary

Candy Land And Unicorns

Candy Land is bright
It is always safe in the night
No need to fear
Princess is always near
Candy Land is fun
You can always relax in the sun
Smurfs dance around unicorns
Almost getting stabbed by their horns
Candy Land is sweet
There's nothing as horrible as wheat
Unicorns are cuddly and pink
Is this a dream, do you think?

Tiyanna Vanessa Lee (9)
Wisbech St Mary CE (VA) Primary School, St Mary

Candyland Poem

Candyland is a huge place
Bigger than outer space
The sweets are so yummy
They're filling up my tummy
Gummies are yummy
Dummies are scrummy
Lucky gummies so yummy
Ta-da.

All my favourite sweets are here
Cadbury chocolate and cookie dough near
A fountain of coke to drink
I float but never sink.

Katelynn New (9)
Wisbech St Mary CE (VA) Primary School, St Mary

Creepy Lego Land

Every night I dream of being in Lego Land
I go on every ride and eat everything

Suddenly, a goat came out of a van
He gave me a thousand pounds each day
Then more and more money

I saw a thousand massive stacks everywhere
Even in the car park
They move when I am not looking at them.

Kalten McCarthy (9)
Wisbech St Mary CE (VA) Primary School, St Mary

In Car Land

In Car Land it's great, you can drive any car
It might even be a plate
The best part is for a licence there is no need
Drive like a beast and speed, speed, speed!

Drive anywhere, if you crash, don't care
As it's a dream you can't die!
So don't be a wimp, give Car Land a try.

Max Waling (8)
Wisbech St Mary CE (VA) Primary School, St Mary

Candyland

One day in Candy Land
A fluffy, amazing unicorn came to Candy Land
It ate all of the candy

There was no candy left but it grew back
And the unicorn kept eating it every day,
The unicorn saw a candy cane.

The unicorn found a castle with a sign that said: *Don't Eat.*

Rhys Parrin (9)
Wisbech St Mary CE (VA) Primary School, St Mary

Roblox Pokémon Go Land Dream

Roblox Pokémon Go Land Dream is a nice place
There are soft Pokémon
Some Pokémon live with Roblox people
Hey, I'm Justin, this is my buddy, Pikachu
Today it is a bright sunny day
I have lots of Pokémon
My favourite is Greninja
This dream is my best!

Justin Ball (9)
Wisbech St Mary CE (VA) Primary School, St Mary

Candy Land

In my candy land I could eat trees and jelly beans
As I sleep I peep
In the sun is fun, I go to the park
The sun is fun
On the slide, I glide
As I hum I eat sweets and I say, 'Yum.'
I go home and say I'm tired
Candy is yum
I went to the shop and bought more candy.

Freddie Dearlove (9)
Wisbech St Mary CE (VA) Primary School, St Mary

Est.1991

YOUNG WRITERS INFORMATION

We hope you have enjoyed reading this book – and that you will continue to in the coming years.

If you're a young writer who enjoys reading and creative writing, or the parent of an enthusiastic poet or story writer, do visit our website **www.youngwriters.co.uk**. Here you will find free competitions, workshops and games, as well as recommended reads, a poetry glossary and our blog.

If you would like to order further copies of this book, or any of our other titles, then please give us a call or visit **www.youngwriters.co.uk**.

Young Writers
Remus House
Coltsfoot Drive
Peterborough
PE2 9BF
(01733) 890066
info@youngwriters.co.uk